Peepers

6.9.14 ♥ your Peeper pal,
Sandy Pugh

Also by Sandy Pugh

A Peeper in My Pocket — A Zany Peep at the ABC's
I Say, You Say — A Zany Peep at Opposites
Meet Me at the Masterpiece — A Zany Peep at Art
BubbleCubes — A Zany Peep at Shapes

Edited by Dana Clerkin

Passports and Postcards

A Zany Trip Around The World

Written & Illustrated

by

Sandy Pugh

Dedicated to
the adventurous spirit
in us all...

Passport

Grab your passport; pack your bags;
We're going to take a trip
All around this great big world
By train and plane and ship!

Learn different ways
to say "hello"
From lands both far and near.
Send postcards
to a friend you know,
"Wishing you were here!"

See
the wonders
of the world
North, South, East, and West.
You're invited; come along
And be the Peepers' guest!

Cheerio!

In jolly old England,
Crumpet, scones, and tea.
Stonehenge forms a circle
An ancient mystery.

Stonehenge was built
4,500 years ago.

It is estimated that it took
30 million hours to build,
and no one knows why...

Bonjour!

Next stop is Paris,

Croissants and eclairs.

Climb the Eiffel Tower;

Be brave and take the stairs!

The Eiffel Tower is the tallest building in Paris. It was built in 1889 and was supposed to be temporary. C'est la vie!

Goddag!

Copenhagen's charming harbor,

A mermaid sits alone.

Thanks to H. C. Andersen

A stone became her throne.

"The Little Mermaid" is a fairy tale written by Hans Christian Andersen who also wrote "Thumbelina" & "The Ugly Duckling."

Ciao!

Travel on to Italy,
Pizza! Pasta! Cheesa!
Catch the Leaning Tower
In the town of Pisa!

"Pisa Pushers" are tourists who take photographs that look like they are holding up the Tower of Pisa.

Buon giorno!

Rome is the home
To the Colosseum.
Gladiators and lions,
I'd rather see than be 'em!

The Colosseum was originally
used for gladiator contests
and animal hunts featuring
zebras, hippos, lions,
tigers, ostriches,
giraffes
and rhinos.

Geia sou!

On a hill in Athens,
A temple to Athena.
The Parthenon with columns tall,
A fitting Greek arena.

Originally, a statue of
Athena, approximately 40
feet high, stood in the
center. She was made of
gold and elephant ivory
Sadly, she is no longer the

Salam!

In the sands of Egypt,

A Sphinx without a nose.

Pyramids and mummies

Pharaohs strike a pose.

What exactly is the Sphinx?

It's a half human, half lion creature built over 4,500 years ago.

Privyet!

Red Square in Russia,
St. Basil's calls it home.
Swirling vibrant colors
On painted onion domes.

"Ivan the Terrible"
built
the Cathedral of St. Basil
in 1552.

Namaste!

Marble, mosques, and minarets,
Elephants pulling carts.
The Taj Mahal in India
A monument of the heart.

More than 1,000 elephants transported building materials for the Taj Mahal. It took 22 years to build. An emperor had it built as a gift for his true love.

Chum reap suor!

The jungles of Cambodia
Are dense and hot and steamy.
A vision, the temple Angkor Wat:
You might just think
you're dreaming.

What is a "wat"?

A temple or monastary in Thailand or Cambodia.

Ni hao

China – land of fireworks,

Pandas, rice, and tea.

The Great Wall stretches

on and on

As far as you can see!

The Great Wall is the largest manmade structure in the world measuring 13,070 miles!

(It is a myth that it can be seen from the moon.)

G'day!

G'day from Down Under!
Koalas and kangaroos
See the Sydney Opera House;
Hop aboard a harbor cruise!

What does the Sydney Opera House look like to you?

Iorana!

Moai on Easter Island,

No bunnies or jelly beans.

880 statues

Looking out to sea.

A Dutch sea captain named the island off the coast of Chile "Easter Island"

because he discovered it on Easter Day 1722.

Moai is pronounced "mo-eye".

Hola!

Lost and found!
In the mountains of Peru.
Our link-a to the Incas;
It's Machu Picchu.

"Machu Picchu" means "old peak".
It is often called the "Lost City of the Incas."

Machu Picchu

Howdy!

Mt. Rushmore's in the U.S.A.

Four presidents in the sun:

Lincoln, Teddy, Jefferson, and

Of course, George Washington.

Each President's head is as tall as a 6-story building!

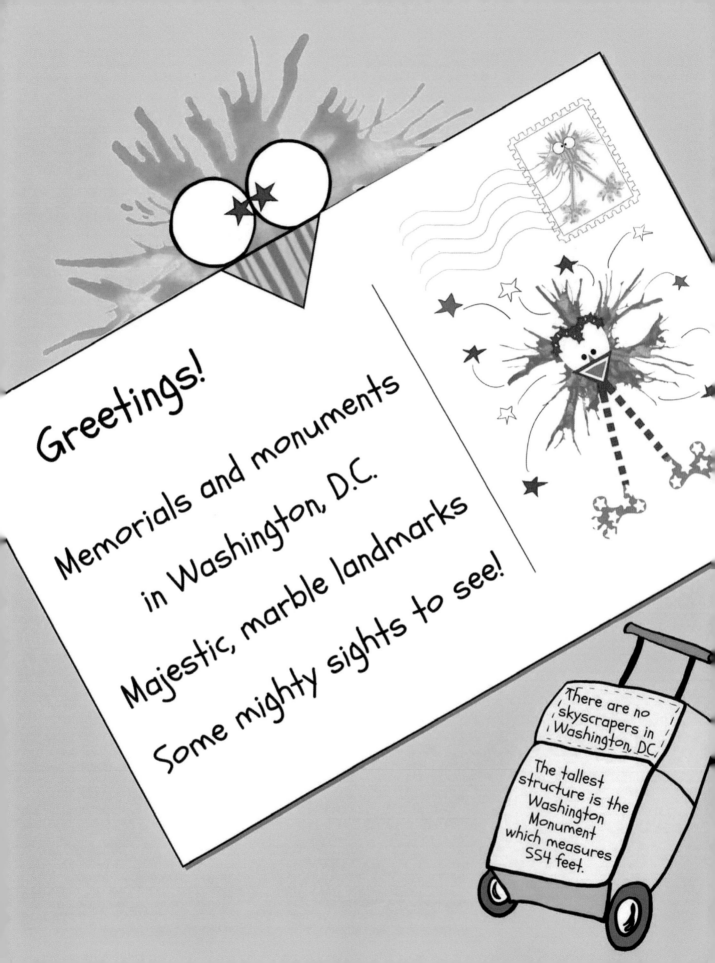

Greetings!

Memorials and monuments
in Washington, D.C.

Majestic, marble landmarks

Some mighty sights to see!

There are no skyscrapers in Washington, D.C.

The tallest structure is the Washington Monument which measures 554 feet.

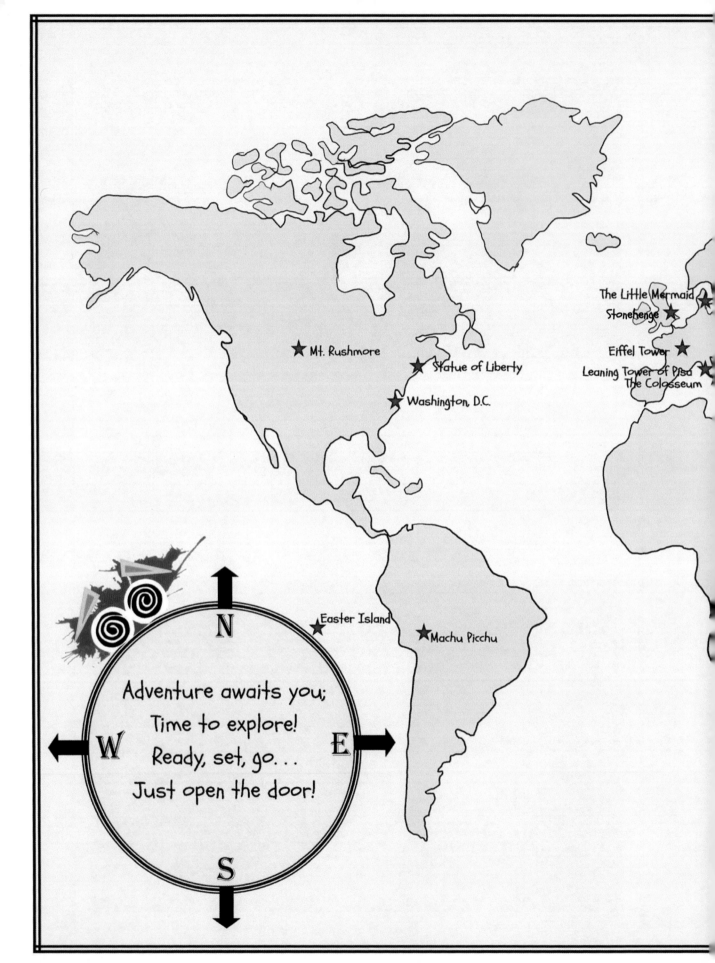

The Little Mermaid
Stonehenge

Mt. Rushmore

Statue of Liberty

Eiffel Tower
Leaning Tower of Pisa
The Colosseum

Washington, D.C.

Easter Island

Machu Picchu

N

W   E

S

Adventure awaits you;
Time to explore!
Ready, set, go. . .
Just open the door!

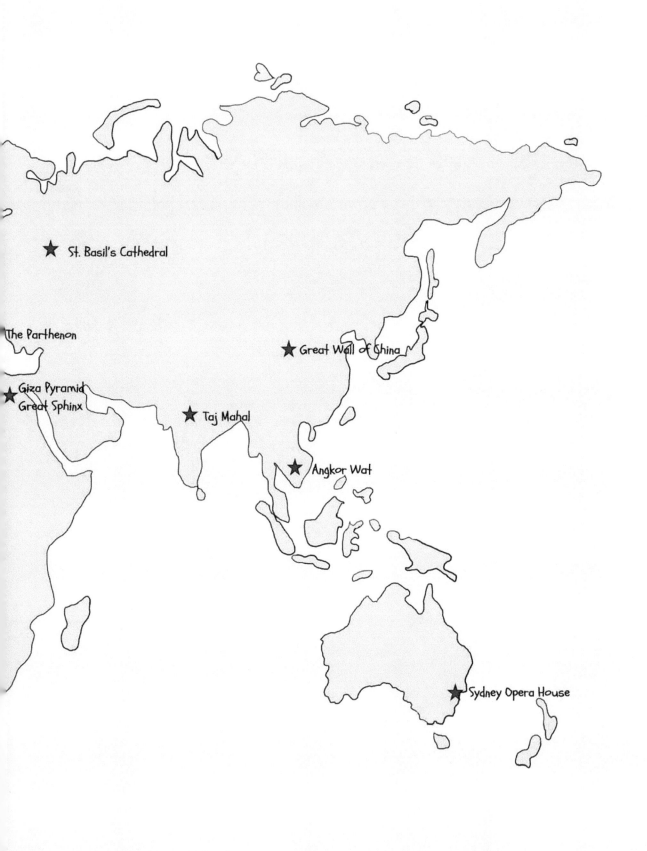

St. Basil's Cathedral

The Parthenon

Giza Pyramid
Great Sphinx

Taj Mahal

Great Wall of China

Angkor Wat

Sydney Opera House

Make your own Peeper!

o Dilute a small amount of tempera paint with a several drops of water.

o With a spoon or your straw, place a small amount of the paint in the center of white paper (enough to make a little puddle).

o With your straw, practice blowing out, NOT IN!

o Blow the paint across the paper – turning the paper to allow the paint to spread out in all directions.

o TAKE A BREAK! Just blow the paint a couple of times and then rest.

o Add more paint if you need to and continue blowing the paint to spread it until you are happy with your Peeper's body.

o While the paint is drying, design your Peeper's eyes, beak and legs.

o Use colored paper to cut out big eyes, a yellow and orange striped beak in the shape of a triangle, and crazy legs with wacky feet. Try a hole punch for polka dots and fancy scissors.

o Once the paint is dry, glue your Peeper parts to your Peeper's body.

o Use your imagination and have FUN!

About the Author and Illustrator

We The Peepers is a company featuring the original work of artist and art teacher, Sandy Pugh. While teaching summer art camp, Sandy created the first whimsical Peeper creatures using a straw, paint and cut paper. <u>Passports and Postcards: A Zany Trip Around the World</u> is Sandy's fifth book in her series. Educators and reading specialists agree that her first two books <u>A Peeper in My Pocket</u> and <u>I Say...You Say...</u> are the ideal books for toddlers and preschoolers. <u>Meet Me at the Masterpiece</u> presents fourteen iconic works of art and draws upon Sandy's background in art appreciation and art history. Laughs abound in her fourth book, <u>BubbleCubes</u>, a wacky look at everyday shapes.

She is the mother of three grown children, Conor, Carey and Austin, and currently lives in Vienna, VA and Oriental, NC with Jimmy, her husband of 33 years.

Made in the USA
Charleston, SC
16 August 2013